HEY AI, WHAT'S UP?

ADHYAYAN TIWARI

To every curious mind that ever wondered, "How does it work?" — and to those brave enough to build the answers.
This book is for you.

Contents

Foreword

In a world where Artificial Intelligence is reshaping every field, it's easy to feel overwhelmed by complexity. But Adhyayan Tiwari brings a refreshing perspective: AI can be fun, human, and accessible for everyone.

"Hey AI, What's Up?" is not just a beginner's guide—it's a bridge between imagination and innovation. With humor, heart, and real-world examples, Adhyayan turns intimidating ideas into stepping stones for the next generation of creators.

Whether you're a student, a dreamer, or someone simply curious about the future, this book offers the perfect starting point. Dive in—you'll be surprised how much you can build when you start with the right question.

Preface

Before I knew what Artificial Intelligence even meant, I was already obsessed with it.

Not with complicated math or coding... but with a blue robot cat named Doraemon.

I grew up watching Doraemon pull wild, futuristic gadgets from his four-dimensional pocket to help his friend Nobita survive school, life, and pure chaos.

And as a kid, I used to wonder:

"What if I could build something like that?"

That curiosity never left me.

Over time, it transformed from sketching gadgets on paper to actually learning about AI — the real-world magic that powers the technology around us.

I wrote Hey AI, What's Up? to make sure no curious mind feels like AI is too complicated or out of reach.

Because imagination isn't just for cartoons. It's for building the future.

Acknowledgements

Writing "Hey AI, What's Up?" has been a journey of passion, learning, and countless late nights fueled by imagination (and maybe a little too much curiosity).

I would like to express my heartfelt gratitude to everyone who inspired me to turn complex ideas about Artificial Intelligence into simple, fun, and relatable conversations — especially for the next generation of creators, dreamers, and builders.

A special thank you to the incredible community of learners around the world who made me believe that education can be exciting, playful, and powerful at the same time.

I am deeply thankful to the tools that made this project possible:
All images and visual illustrations in this book have been generated using ChatGPT's AI-powered image generation tools.
They are designed to make learning not just easier, but also more colorful and memorable.

Finally, to every reader who picked up this book with curiosity —
I see you, I believe in you, and I can't wait to see what you build next. ?
This is just the beginning.

Let's go change the world — one idea, one experiment, one dream at a time.

Prologue

Imagine a world where machines don't just follow instructions —
they learn, adapt, and even surprise us.

That world isn't tomorrow.
It's today.

Artificial Intelligence is no longer a distant dream from sci-fi movies.
It's in your phone, your playlists, your photos, and your conversations.\n>

Hey AI, What's Up? isn't about overwhelming you with technical jargon.
It's about giving you the keys to understanding, creating, and exploring AI for yourself.

The future belongs to those who ask questions, who stay curious, and who dare to build.\n>
Are you ready to meet the world of AI not as a stranger, but as a new friend?\n>
Let's dive in.

Welcome to the World of AI

"It all starts with a question: What if machines could think like us?"

Get ready to explore how AI was born, how it lives around you, and how it's already shaping the future you live in.

Let's unlock the basics of intelligence — human and artificial.

CHAPTER I

Wait... What Is AI, Actually?

How It All Began: A Very Human History of AI

"Before AI could beat humans at chess, it had to learn how to play checkers."
Let's rewind the tech clock

1950s: The OG Dreamers

It all started with humans asking a big question: "Can machines think?"
Cue Alan Turing, a British codebreaker and computer wizard, who proposed the now-famous Turing Test:
If a machine can hold a conversation indistinguishable from a human, is it thinking?

In 1956, a bunch of brilliant nerds met at Dartmouth College and basically said:

"Let's build intelligent machines."
That meeting is now known as the official birth of Artificial Intelligence.

1960s–70s: Rule-Based AI (aka If-This-Then-That)

These early AIs didn't learn. They followed rules.
You gave them conditions: "If rainy, bring umbrella." They gave you logical responses. They worked okay... but couldn't handle real-world messiness.

1980s: Expert Systems

AI took a glow-up. "Expert Systems" were designed to mimic how doctors or engineers make decisions.
Cool idea, but they:

- Needed tons of human-written rules
- Broke down fast when things got complicated

1997: The First Mic-Drop

IBM's Deep Blue beats chess legend Garry Kasparov.
A machine had officially beaten a world champion. Minds were blown.

2012–Now: The Deep Learning Revolution

This is where things exploded. AI stopped following rules and It started learning from data

With GPUs, big data, and brain-like networks (hello, deep learning), AI suddenly got really good

Today: AI is Everywhere

From your camera roll to your favorite playlist to the robots in hospitals—AI has gone mainstream.

And this is just the beginning

So... What Is AI, Actually?

Let's get one thing straight:

AI isn't just about robots doing backflips or creepy machines plotting world domination.

It's not even all about coding (yet).

At its core, Artificial Intelligence is when machines are built to do things that usually need human smarts. Stuff like:

- Learning from experience
- Solving problems
- Understanding language
- Recognizing patterns
- Making decisions

In short:

AI = Machines that can "think" (kinda) like us.

But here's the cool part: AI isn't just for tech geniuses or secret labs. You're already using it. Like... a lot.

Where You've Already Met AI

Everyday Things	The AI Behind It
Google Photos	Computer Vision
Siri/alexa/ ChatGPT	NLP
Instagram	Machine Learning
Snapchat Filters	Facial Detection AI

"You thought AI was a science fair project. Turns out, it's been stalking you online all day."

But Wait—AI ≠ Magic

Let's bust a myth real quick.
AI doesn't "think" like a human. It doesn't feel.
It doesn't want things. (Unless you count wanting more data.)
It's just super smart math and algorithms trained on huge amounts of information.
So instead of giving it step-by-step instructions like a normal computer, you let it learn from patterns and examples.
Kinda like how you learned what a cat is:

- Saw enough cats
- Figured out "okay they're fluffy, small, and slightly evil"
- Now you recognize them instantly

AI does the same. Except faster. Way faster. Like... millions-of-images-a-second fast.

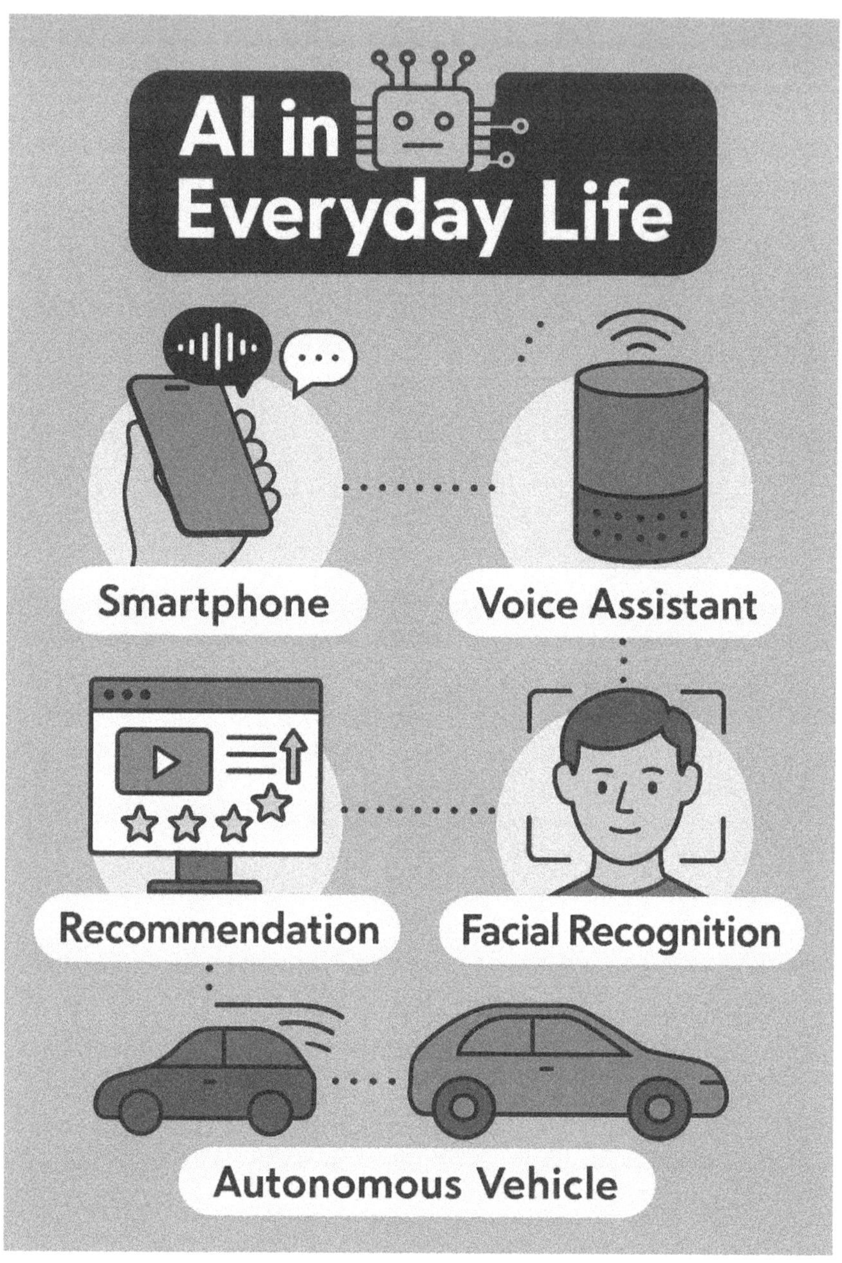
AI in
Everyday Life
Smartphone
Voice Assistant
Recommendation
Facial Recognition
Autonomous Vehicle

How AI Actually Learns Stuff (And Why It's a Bit Like Training a Dog... or a Toddler on Sugar)

Alright, real talk. When people hear "AI learns things," their brain often goes "Wait... HOW?! Machines don't have brains or feelings or coffee addictions. So what do you mean they learn?"

Well buckle up, because we're diving into the world of machine learning — the heart and squishy soul of AI.

First of All... What Is Learning?

Whether you're a golden retriever, a three-year-old child, or a machine — learning is basically: Getting better at something through experience.

- Humans? We learn by trying stuff, failing, trying again, maybe crying a little, and then slowly figuring it out.
- Machines? Same vibe. Less crying. More math.

Machine Learning 101: The Baby Steps

Imagine you want a computer to tell the difference between pictures of cats and dogs.

You could write a billion rules like:

- "Cats have pointy ears."
- "Dogs sometimes wear bandanas."
- "If it's judging you silently, it's a cat."

But that's exhausting and honestly doesn't work well. So instead, we do this:

Step 1: Give It Data (Like, A LOT of It)

We feed the AI a bunch of labeled examples:

- "This is a cat."
- "This is a dog."
- Repeat x 10,000 (or 10 million if you're Google).

Step 2: The AI Tries to Spot Patterns

It starts looking for common stuff:

- "Hmm, cats often have triangle-shaped ears."
- "Dogs? Maybe longer snouts?"
- "Oh no, what's a Chihuahua???"

Step 3: It Makes Guesses... Then Gets Corrected

It guesses: "This one's a dog!"
You go: "Nope, that's a cat, buddy."

And the AI adjusts its inner math (literally tweaking numbers in a big matrix of weights and biases — like tuning a massive radio station).

Repeat this millions of times... and boom, it learns.

Wait... Why Is This Like Training a Dog?

Glad you asked.

Human Stuff	Dog Training	AI Learning
Repetition	Sit, stay, roll over again and again	Feed it millions of examples
Rewards	Treats! (and belly rubs)	Accuracy goes up! (yay data)
Corrections	"No, bad dog!"	"Nope, wrong answer, adjust weights!"
Progress	Learns to fetch	Learns to recognize cats

Now imagine training a super-hyper toddler on Red Bull, who keeps guessing wrong but never stops trying. That's your average early-stage AI model.

Quick Brain Break: What's Actually Happening Inside?

Okay so inside the AI, what's going on is a lot of this:

- **Input:** A bunch of numbers (yes, your cat pic becomes numbers)
- **Processing:** These numbers go through something called a neural network (don't worry, we'll talk about that later — it's basically fake brain stuff).
- **Output:** A guess — like "80% sure this is a dog."
- **Feedback:** If it's wrong, it adjusts using a method called backpropagation (fancy word alert! Basically: fix the mistake and try again).

This cycle goes on a bajillion times until it's so good at guessing that it can do it with brand-new data it's never seen before.

But Here's the Catch...

AI isn't magic. If you feed it garbage data (or biased data), it will learn garbage things.

It's like if you only showed a dog photos of golden retrievers and said, "This is what ALL dogs look like." Now it thinks chihuahuas are aliens.

Good data = smart AI.

Bad data = derpy robot with confidence issues.

Meet the Learning Styles of AI

Okay, so imagine trying to teach a dog to do a backflip. You don't sit him down with a textbook. You show him, reward him, repeat a million times, and hope he doesn't run off chasing a squirrel. ?

AI's kinda like that—but with math instead of treats.

There are 3 Big Ways AI Learns:

1. Supervised Learning

TL;DR(Too Lazy?; Don't Read): You show the AI stuff + tell it what it is.

This is like teaching with flashcards:

- "This is a cat."
- "This is a dog."
- "No, that's your foot. Not a potato."

Once the AI sees enough examples, it starts recognizing patterns and making predictions.

Used in:

- Spam detection in emails
- Facial recognition
- Weather predictions

Real-Life Vibe: Like a teacher guiding you every step of the way (with answer keys and red pens).

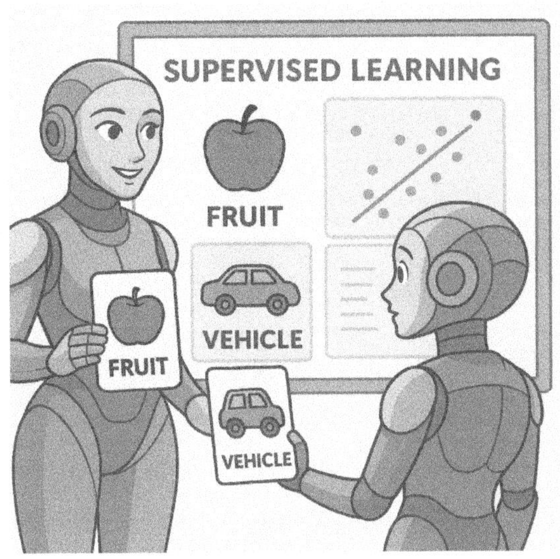

2. Unsupervised Learning

TL;DR: You don't tell the AI anything. It figures stuff out on its own.

No labels. No instructions. Just raw, messy data.

The AI's job? Spot patterns. Group things that look similar. Basically play detective with zero context. Used in:

- Customer segmentation for marketing
- Organizing photos by similarity
- Discovering unknown trends

Real-Life Vibe: Like dumping a toddler into a Lego pile and seeing what they build. No instructions, just chaos and creativity.

3. Reinforcement Learning

TL;DR: You give the AI a goal. It tries, fails, learns, and gets better. Think of it like training a video game bot. The AI gets:

- A goal
- A reward when it does well
- A penalty when it messes up

Over time, it figures out what actions lead to max rewards.
Used in:

- Self-driving cars
- Game-playing AIs (like AlphaGo)
- Robotics (a.k.a. teaching a robot to not walk into walls)

Real-Life Vibe: Like teaching a kid to play Mario Kart by letting them crash a lot first. Then cheer when they finally win a race.

Welcome to the Modelverse

(A.K.A. The Different Brains of AI — From Lazy Geniuses to Deep Thinkers)

Imagine a whole classroom of AI students. Each one learns in a slightly different way. Some are fast but make mistakes. Some are slow but super deep. And some... well, some are basically magic.

Here's your VIP pass to meet the squad

1. Linear Regression:

The Chill Math Nerd

Best For: Predicting things with a straight-line relationship

Brain Style: "Keep it simple. One line fits all."

Used in: Predicting prices, trends, or scores

Think: "If you study more hours, your grade probably goes up."

Just a nice clean line that says, "More X = More Y." No drama.

2. Decision Trees:

The "Choose Your Own Adventure" Brain
  Best For: When you want the AI to make decisions like "if this, then that"
Brain Style: "Let's break this down into tiny, logical steps."
Used in: Loan approval, medical diagnoses, sorting stuff
  Like a giant flowchart. "Is it raining? Yes → Take an umbrella. No →
Sunglasses time."

3. Logistic Regression:

The Yes/No Guy
  Best For: Binary decisions (this or that?)
Brain Style: "I'm either confident or I'm not."
Used in: Email spam detection, predicting if someone will click a link
  It doesn't care about shades of gray. Just yes or no. 1 or 0. Friend or foe.

4. Neural Networks:

The Deep Thinker (Like, Really Deep)
  Best For: Complex stuff like image recognition, speech, natural language
Brain Style: "Let me think... deeper... deeper... ah yes."
Used in: Self-driving cars, facial recognition, ChatGPT
  Inspired by the human brain (but way faster and not addicted to
caffeine).
Each "neuron" connects to others in layers and learns patterns by adjusting
connections—like a brain, but 100% silicon.

5. K-Means Clustering:

The Pattern Spotter Without Instructions
  Best For: Grouping similar things with no labels
Brain Style: "You guys kinda look the same. You go over here."
Used in: Customer segmentation, image compression
  Like organizing your playlist by vibes instead of genres

6. *Support Vector Machines (SVM):*

The Perfectionist
Best For: Drawing sharp boundaries between things
Brain Style: "Let me draw the best possible line. Like, THE BEST."
Used in: Face detection, classification tasks
Basically the neat freak of the AI world. Draws a perfect divider and dares anyone to cross it.

7. *Random Forests:*

The Decision Tree Party
Best For: Accuracy without overthinking
Brain Style: "Let's ask a bunch of decision trees and vote on the answer."
Used in: Predictions, classification, risk assessment
Like a group project where everyone does their job, then agrees on the best answer. For once.

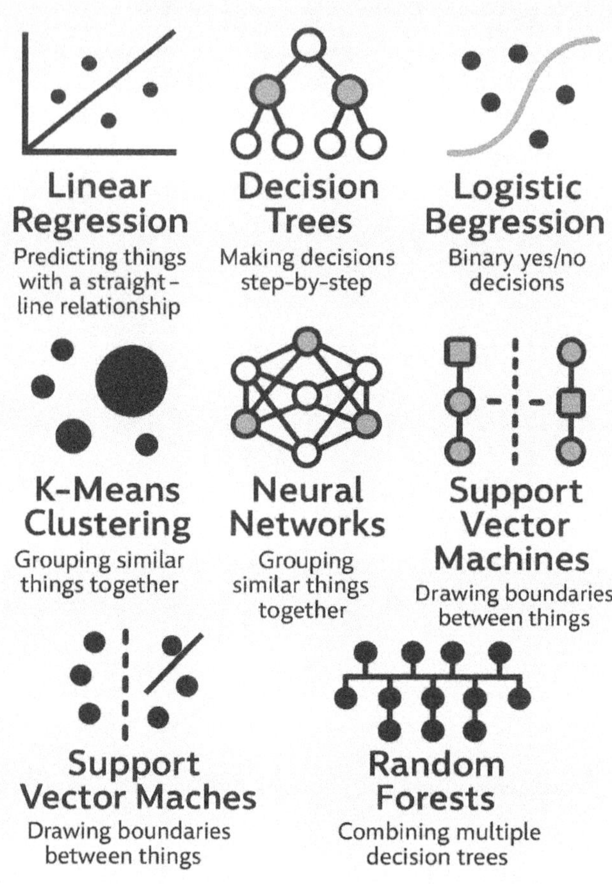

Prepping Data: AI's Cooking Show

Before any AI model can get cooking, it needs clean, clear, and tasty data. Think of data prep like washing vegetables, peeling potatoes, and slicing onions before the cooking starts.

What's Data Prep Actually Look Like?

- Cleaning: Tossing out garbage data (duplicates, mistakes, weird glitches)

- Formatting: Making sure data is consistent (like dates in the same format)
- Labeling: Clearly marking data (this pic = dog, this email = spam)
- Splitting: Dividing data into Training, Testing, and Validation sets: Training Data (AI learns from this), Testing Data (AI gets tested here), Validation Data (Double-checking final results)

Real-life vibe: Like prepping ingredients carefully to make sure your meal doesn't end up tasting like soap.

| Good Data = Good AI, Garbage In = Disaster Out

Ever tried cooking a delicious meal with rotten ingredients? Yeah, it doesn't work so great. Same rule applies here:

| Garbage In, Garbage Out (GIGO)

If your AI learns from biased or inaccurate data, it'll end up biased or inaccurate too.

For example:

- Bad facial recognition data → AI misidentifies people (big oof)
- Biased hiring data → AI discriminates against groups (bigger oof)

Bottom line: Great AI needs carefully collected, balanced, diverse data—just like good cooking needs fresh, high-quality ingredients.

Leveling Up Your AI (a.k.a. Training the Model)

Ever played a video game and grinded levels until your character was unbeatable? That's exactly how AI training works.

- Start Small: AI makes random guesses at first.
- Get Feedback: Every wrong guess helps AI tweak itself (backpropagation for neural networks, parameter tuning for simpler models).
- Improve: The AI gradually reduces mistakes (like gaining XP after every battle).

This improvement is measured using metrics like:

- Accuracy (how often it guesses right)

- Precision & Recall (how good is it at finding and correctly identifying stuff)
- Loss function (the lower the number, the better!)

After training for millions of rounds, AI gets scary good at what it's meant to do—spotting cancer cells, recommending TikTok videos, or driving safely (usually!)

Good AI isn't magic—it's math + careful data + practice. Models don't start off smart; they become smart. And behind every AI success story is someone who took data seriously, prepped it right, and patiently leveled up their digital companion.

CHAPTER III

Yo AI, Do You Even Speak Human??

Natural Language Processing, Explained Without the Jargon

Ever wondered how ChatGPT casually writes your English essay in 5 minutes flat, while it takes you hours?

Or how Spotify somehow knows your exact music mood when you type something super vague like "chill vibes for studying, but not boring"?

Maybe you've even noticed how Instagram captions and TikTok subtitles appear automatically—shockingly accurate (usually), even when you mumble?

That, my friend, is Natural Language Processing (NLP).

First: What the Heck is NLP?

In the simplest terms, NLP is AI learning to understand, interpret, and generate human language.

No big deal, right? Except human language is ridiculously complicated:

We've got sarcasm, slang, emojis , weird grammar rules, and phrases like "break a leg" meaning "good luck" instead of "please injure yourself."

AI somehow has to decode all of that.

How NLP Actually Works

NLP teaches computers language by breaking down words into pieces and patterns.

Imagine a robot trying to understand this text:

"I love pizza "

Here's what happens inside the AI's digital brain:

Step 1: Tokenization

Breaking text into words: "I", "love", "pizza"

Step 2: Part-of-Speech (POS) Tagging

Figuring out what each word does:

"I" = pronoun

"love" = verb

"pizza" = noun

Step 3: Understanding Context

Pizza is food. "Love" means the person enjoys it a lot. The emoji reinforces positivity.

Step 4: Generating Response

Maybe the AI suggests pizza delivery ads next. (Sneaky AI marketing)

NLP in Real Life: Where You've Already Seen It

- Siri / Alexa :Voice recognition and responses
- Google Translate: Translating languages in seconds
- Grammarly: Grammar checking, style suggestions
- ChatGPT: Answering almost anything
- Spam Detection:Identifying suspicious language

Why NLP is Tricky (A.K.A. Why AI Sometimes Says Weird Stuff)

Remember when AI gave super weird answers, or misunderstood your voice command? That's because NLP isn't perfect yet. It struggles with:

- Ambiguity: "Let's eat grandma" vs. "Let's eat, grandma." Commas literally save lives.
- Sarcasm: "Oh sure, I love doing homework all weekend." (Humans get sarcasm; AI, not always.)

Large Language Models (like GPT) — How They Work & Why They're Powerful

Imagine you had a super brain that read basically the entire internet. Every book, article, Reddit thread, and meme. That's kind of what a language model is—especially the big ones like GPT (Generative Pre-trained Transformer).

What Is a Language Model?

A language model is an AI system trained to:

- Understand human language
- Predict the next word in a sentence
- Write, answer, summarize, translate, or even joke (sort of)

It doesn't "think" like humans—it doesn't know facts like we do—but it's ridiculously good at using patterns in language to create realistic, intelligent-sounding responses.

How Does GPT Work? (Simplified)

- Trained on Massive Text Data: It reads trillions of words from books, websites, news, chats, and more to learn grammar, style, facts, slang, etc.
- Uses the Transformer Architecture: Transformers are like supercharged attention systems. They help the AI focus on what parts of a sentence or paragraph matter most for meaning.

Example:

"He didn't go because he was tired."
The model uses attention to figure out who "he" is and what "because" refers to.
   #Predicts the Next Word
Given a prompt like "I went to the store to buy some...", the model guesses: milk"? "candy"? "explosives"?
Based on what's most likely and what makes the most sense in context.

Why Are LLMs Like GPT So Powerful?

They Understand Context: Unlike older AI that just matched keywords, GPT understands meaning across long passages.

They Can Be Creative: They write poems, scripts, stories, jokes, or rants in almost any tone or style.

They're Versatile: GPT can switch between:

- science tutor
- A coding assistant
- A writing coach
- A sarcastic chatbot

They Learn Indirectly from People: Through their training data, they pick up how people talk, argue, explain, and express emotion.

But GPT Isn't Perfect

It doesn't truly "know" facts—sometimes it makes stuff up. It can sound confident even when it's wrong (called hallucination). It doesn't understand feelings—it just mimics them.

That's why it's important to use it wisely, always double-check what it says, and never treat it like a real person.

When GPT Overthinks Like a Tired College Student

(Yes, even AI spirals sometimes...)

You

Reasoned about what I do for 6 seconds ⌄

Okay, so the user just said "You." Hmm, this is a little ambiguous—maybe they're asking about me, "What do you do?" but that doesn't quite fit since we were just talking. Maybe they're being a little snarky, or just trying to keep the convo going. I'll go with something like "I'm ChatGPT, your AI assistant! I'm here to help you with anything you need—whether it's chatting, answering your questions, or just bouncing around some ideas. Let's have fun with it!" That sounds fun, right?

Alright, I'm thinking I'll keep it casual and friendly. The user didn't ask anything specific, so I'll break it down in a fun, laid-back way. Maybe something like: "I do tons of stuff! From answering your questions to chatting and even making up goofy jokes. I'm here to help however I can, and if you want to be playful or serious, I've got your back. Think of me like your AI sidekick, always ready to chat!" That feels just right—talkative but still clear!

I'm your friendly AI sidekick—kind of like a digital Swiss Army knife for conversation! I'm here to answer questions, chat about anything from the quirky to the profound, and help out with whatever you need. Think of me as your 24/7 buddy who can dish out trivia, brainstorming sessions, goofy jokes, or even some life advice when you need it. How can I help brighten your day today?

So yeah, GPT is smart... but it's also a little dramatic sometimes. Kinda relatable, *right*?

CHAPTER IV

Can AI See Me?

Computer Vision and the Magic of Machine Sight

Imagine your phone unlocking when it sees your face, Snapchat filters sticking to your head like they're glued, or cars driving themselves through traffic without crashing (hopefully).

That's not just tech wizardry.

That's Computer Vision — AI's eyes.

What Is Computer Vision?

Computer Vision (CV) is the field of AI that teaches machines how to "see" the world, understand images, and even make decisions based on what they see.

In human terms:

We see something → our brain processes it → we react

In AI terms:

- Camera captures image
- AI analyzes it using trained models
- AI reacts (classifies, detects, tracks, etc.)

You Already Use CV Every Day

- Face ID: Unlocks your phone using your face
- Google Photos: Groups pictures of the same person
- Snapchat Filters: Tracks your face to add effects
- Self-driving Cars: Detects pedestrians, lanes, stop signs
- Amazon Go Stores: Detects what items you take off shelves
- Security Cameras: Detect intruders or unusual behavior

How Does It Work?

Let's simplify it:
    Input = Images or Video
(Still pictures or moving footage from cameras)
    Processing = Feature Extraction
The AI looks for things like:

- Edges
- Shapes
- Colors
- Patterns

    Output = Understanding
The AI says:

- "There's a stop sign."
- "That person looks suspicious."

Real-World Examples That Are Actually Cool

- Tesla's self-driving tech : Uses CV to detect lanes, vehicles, and traffic lights.
- Medical Imaging : AI spots early signs of cancer in scans faster than doctors sometimes can.
- Retail stores like Amazon Go : No cashier, no problem. Cameras + CV = auto checkout.
- Sports broadcasting : AI tracks players and ball movements for replays and analytics.

Wait... Can It See Like a Human?

Kinda. But not really.
    CV doesn't "see" like you and I do.
It breaks images down into numbers (pixels = data) and looks for statistical

patterns using models, especially Convolutional Neural Networks (CNNs).

A CNN is like AI's visual cortex—it sees edges, textures, and builds up a "picture" layer by layer.

We'll break that down in the next part.

CNNs – The Visual Brain of AI

So, machines don't "see" like we do—they see numbers. And Convolutional Neural Networks (CNNs) help them make sense of those numbers, one layer at a time.

Think of a CNN like an AI artist that's staring at a pixel painting, squinting real hard to find patterns.

A Convolutional Neural Network is a special kind of neural network designed specifically to Analyze visual data.

How It Works (Step-by-Step Breakdown):

1. Input Layer

You upload an image (say, a dog photo). The image is turned into pixel values (numbers, basically).

2. Convolution Layer

This is where CNN uses filters (small matrices) to scan the image. These filters detect features like edges, textures, and corners.

It's like holding a magnifying glass over the image and looking for sharp changes in color and light.

3. ReLU Activation

This layer throws out all the "negative energy" (negative values) and keeps only the strong signals. Think of it like "Yeah, ignore the noise. Let's focus on what pops."

4. Pooling Layer

This downsizes the image. It keeps the important info but throws away unnecessary details. Makes the network faster, smarter, and less overwhelmed.

Kinda like cropping out the boring background in a photo.

5. Flatten Layer

All that image data is flattened into a single line of numbers. This is the final summary of what the network has seen.

6. Fully Connected Layer

This is where decision-making happens. The flattened numbers are fed into a classic neural network that says:

- "Yep, that's a dog."
- "Nope, that's a cat."
- "Hmm... is that a loaf of bread or a puppy?"

Why CNNs Are So Effective?

- They don't get confused by background noise.
- They're fast, scalable, and great at pattern recognition.

- They work better on images than regular neural nets because they focus on spatial relationships (how pixels relate to each other).

Layer by layer, they go from:

"This looks like an edge" → "This looks like a nose" → "This is probably a dog's face."

CHAPTER V

Deep Learning — When AI Gets, Well... Deep

If machine learning is teaching a toddler with flashcards, then deep learning is like giving that toddler a superbrain and letting them figure things out with billions of examples.

What's Deep Learning?

Deep Learning is a part of machine learning that uses neural networks with multiple layers — so many layers, it's "deep."

It's how:

- Siri understands your voice
- ChatGPT generates human-like responses
- Tesla's autopilot sees the road
- Google Photos magically finds all your dog pics
- Midjourney, Sora and DALL·E turn words into stunning images

How It's Built?

Deep Learning models are based on Artificial Neural Networks (ANNs) — networks inspired by the human brain.

Each layer is made of neurons (math-y ones, not squishy ones) that pass info to each other, learn patterns, and tweak themselves to get better.

The more layers = the deeper the learning = the smarter the network (usually).

Types of Deep Learning Models and their Uses

- Feedforward Neural Network (FNN): Basic tasks like image recognition
- Convolutional Neural Network (CNN): Image data & computer vision (already covered!)

- Recurrent Neural Network (RNN): Time-based sequences like speech or stock prices
- LSTM (Long Short-Term Memory): Remembering long sequences (great for text + music)
- Transformers: Understanding context in language (used in ChatGPT & BERT)

So Why Use Deep Learning?

Because it can:

- Handle complex problems
- Learn from raw data without much human help
- Beat traditional ML in speech, vision, and language
- Adapt, improve, and evolve over time

The Catch?
Deep learning needs:

- LOTS of data
- LOTS of time
- LOTS of computing power

And sometimes... patience.

You've Officially Entered "The Matrix"

Deep learning is the tech behind today's most advanced AI.
If you've used ChatGPT, seen DeepFakes, watched a self-driving demo, or played with image generators — you've seen deep learning in action.

DEEP LEARNING

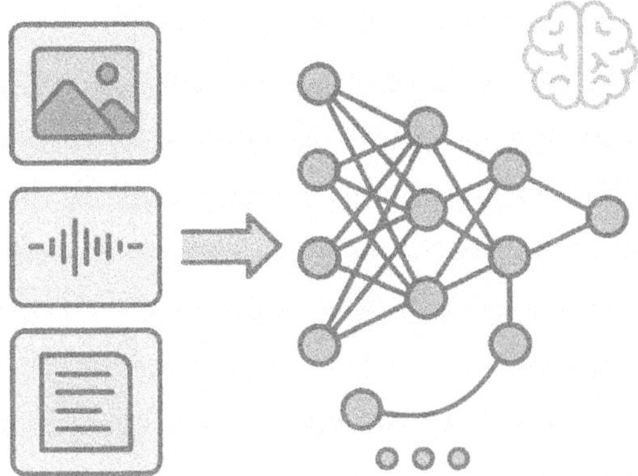

Deep Learning Decoded: The Digital Brain at WorkA vibrant look into how layered neural networks process data, learn patterns, and power everything from voice assistants to self-driving cars.

CHAPTER VI

AI Ethics — The Good, The Bad & The Biased

"Just because AI can do something... doesn't always mean it should."

Now that you know what AI is and how it learns, it's time for a real talk:

"What happens when AI makes decisions that aren't fair? Or when it learns the wrong lessons from the data we give it?"

We Learnt everything but now, It's about responsibility.

Why Do Ethics in AI Even Matter?

Because AI is now used to:

- Approve loans
- Pick job candidates
- Decide prison sentences
- Detect "threats" in public spaces
- Decide who gets into what college

If it's learning from biased, incomplete, or messed-up data — guess what? It repeats the same biases. Just faster. And with confidence.

Real-World AI Fails (That Actually Happened)

1. Facial Recognition Bias

Studies showed that some systems had 99% accuracy for white male faces But only ~65% for Black women That means real people were misidentified, and sometimes even wrongfully arrested.

2. Resume Screening

One company trained AI to pick candidates based on past hires. The problem? Past hires were mostly men. The AI learned: "Hire men. Ignore women." 💀?

3. Content Moderation Bias

AI tools sometimes flag innocent posts in minority languages as "dangerous." Or let hate speech slide if it's phrased a certain way.

Why These Problems Happen?

AI doesn't have morals. It learns from us — from the data we feed it.
If the data is:

* Biased
* Incomplete
* Lacking diversity

...then the AI will be too.
Garbage in = Garbage out. But faster. And automated.

Where You Come In

You don't need a PhD to spot ethical issues. You just need to ask:

* "Who might this hurt?"
* "Is this fair for everyone?"
* "Would I be okay with this if it affected me?"

Being a good AI builder means being a good human first.
And sometimes that means slowing down and asking questions no one else is asking.

Building Trust with Ethical AI ??A simple but powerful reminder: as AI gets smarter, it must also stay fair, transparent, accountable, and respectful of privacy. The future of tech isn't just about what AI can do — but what it should do.

How Do We Fix It?

Here's what ethical AI should aim for:

- Fairness: Don't treat people differently based on race, gender, etc.
- Transparency: Make it clear how decisions are made

- Accountability: Someone needs to take responsibility
- Privacy: Don't steal people's data just because you can
- Explainability: Users should understand why the AI did something

AI doesn't have a conscience. But you do.
And that might be the most important tool in the whole system.

Building with AI — Coding It Yourself

"Knowing is great. But building? That's magic."

Now that you understand what AI is, it's time to get your hands dirty. You'll learn how to talk to data, teach machines, and build real AI projects.

From zero to hero — one line of code at a time.

CHAPTER VII

Python for AI Beginners

Welcome to the part of the book where we go from thinking about AI to actually building it.

We learn how to talk to machines.

And guess what? You don't need Matrix powers or hacker sunglasses for this.

You just need Python.

What's Python, and Why Should You Care?

Python is the language of AI. Like, THE language.

- It's easy to write (no weird semicolons or curly brackets).
- It's super popular (used by Google, NASA, Netflix... and now, you).
- It's got all the tools for AI built right in.

So, if you want to build an AI that writes poems, drives cars, or sorts your memes by vibe—Python's your starting line.

Setting Up Your Python Playground

You've got two ways to start writing Python code:

Option A: Google Colab (best for beginners)

- Runs in your browser
- Nothing to install
- Free access to GPUs (fancy computer power)

Just go to: colab.research.google.com
Create a new notebook, and you're ready.

Option B: Install Python Locally (for rebels & tinkerers)

- Download Python
- Use an editor like VS Code

- Write your code in .py files and run it using your terminal

For this book, we'll assume you're using Google Colab (because it's fast, simple, and you can never "accidentally delete your entire C drive.")

Your First Python Line Ever

Let's break the silence between you and the machine:

```
print("Hey AI, what's up?")
```

This is Python's way of saying hello. Run it. See the response. Feel the power.

Python Basics (That You'll Actually Use)

1. Variables: Storing Stuff

```
name = "Adhyayan" age = 17 fav_ai_topic = "Computer Vision"
```

Think of variables like labeled boxes to store info.

2. Printing Things

```
print("My name is", name)
print("In five years, I'll be", age + 5)
```

3. Lists: Grouping Stuff

```
hobbies = ["coding", "chess", "listening to AI podcasts"]
print(hobbies[0]) # first item
```

4. Loops: Doing Things Again & Again

```
for hobby in hobbies:
    print("One of my hobbies is", hobby)
```

Want to loop something five times?

```
for i in range(5):
print("AI is awesome")
```

5. Conditions: Making Decisions

```
score = 85
    if score > 90:
    print("You crushed it!")
    elif score > 70:
    print("You did great!")
    else:
    print("Let's tweak the model next time.")
```

6. Functions: Your Own Mini-Programs

```
def greet(name):
    print("Hey", name, "ready to build AI?")
    greet("Adhyayan")
```

Functions are blocks of code you can reuse anytime, anywhere. They're your besties.

CHAPTER VIII

Hello, Data!

42

"Let's teach your code to read actual stuff"

You've learned how to write code. But now it's time for your next AI superpower: handling data. Because AI doesn't just run on code—it runs on data.

It's how AI learns:

- What cats look like
- What makes a review positive
- What the weather might be tomorrow

Without data, your code is just… guessing. With data? It's unstoppable. Let's start feeding it.

What Is Data?

Data is information. That's it. It can be:

- Words from a story
- Numbers in a spreadsheet
- Pixels in a photo
- Ratings from your last food order

Machines don't "know" what data means. You have to show them what to do with it.

Reading Text with Python

Let's say you have a file called message.txt that says:
Hello future coder! Welcome to your first text file. AI is hungry for data.

Your Code:

with open("message.txt") as file:

```
content = file.read()
print(content)
```
Output:
Hello future coder! Welcome to your first text file. AI is hungry for data. <u>You just read your first data file.</u>

Mini Mission:

Count how many words are in the file:
```
word_count = len(content.split())
print("Word count:", word_count)
```
This is the foundation of NLP — turning words into something the machine can work with.

Reading Tables (CSV Files)

What's a CSV?

CSV = Comma-Separated Values
It's like a spreadsheet saved as text.
```
Example: books.csv
Title,Author,Rating Dune,Frank Herbert,9 Harry Potter,J.K. Rowling,8
Twilight,Stephenie Meyer,6
```

Your Code (with Pandas):

```
import pandas as pd
df = pd.read_csv("books.csv")
print(df.head()) # Shows the first 5 rows
```

What You Can Do:

```
print("Columns:", df.columns)
print("Average rating:", df["Rating"].mean())
print("Books rated 8 or higher:")
print(df[df["Rating"] >= 8])
```
Boom—you're now doing real data analysis.

Mini Mission: Personal Dataset

Create your own CSV file called my_movies.csv with 3 columns: Movie, Genre, Rating.

Then write code to:

- Show only "Sci-Fi" movies
- Show movies rated above 7
- Calculate the average rating

CHAPTER IX

NLP in Code

Making Machines Read, Write, and Maybe Even Feel

Ever asked Siri to "play chill music" and it totally got you?

Or chatted with a bot that actually made sense?

That's NLP — Natural Language Processing.

And now, it's your turn to build with it.

Tools You'll Need

We'll use:

nltk – the classic NLP toolkit

textblob – great for sentiment analysis

(later) Hugging Face ? – for advanced stuff

Install the Tools (in Colab):

```
!pip install nltk textblob
    import nltk
    nltk.download('punkt')
    nltk.download('averaged_perceptron_tagger')
```

Tokenization – Breaking Text into Words

```
from nltk.tokenize import word_tokenize
    text = "AI is not magic. It's just smart math!"
    tokens = word_tokenize(text)
    print(tokens)
    Output:
    ['AI', 'is', 'not', 'magic', '.', 'It', "'s", 'just', 'smart', 'math', '!']
```

That's called tokenization — splitting text into parts your AI can work with.

Part-of-Speech Tagging

Let's see what type of word each token is:

```
pos = nltk.pos_tag(tokens)
print(pos)
Example output:
[('AI', 'NN'), ('is', 'VBZ'), ('smart', 'JJ'), ('math', 'NN')]
NN = noun
VBZ = verb
JJ = adjective
```

It's like grammar class, but cooler.

Sentiment Analysis with TextBlob

```
from textblob import TextBlob
    blob = TextBlob("I absolutely love this robot!")
    print(blob.sentiment)
```

Output:

```
Sentiment(polarity=0.625, subjectivity=0.6)
    Polarity: -1 = bad , +1 = good
    Subjectivity: 0 = fact, 1 = opinion
    Try it on:
```

- Angry text
- Happy review
- Something neutral

Mini Project: Mood Detector

```
text = input("How are you feeling today? ") blob = TextBlob(text) polarity = blob.sentiment.polarity
    if polarity > 0:
    print("You sound happy! ")
    elif polarity < 0:
    print("Hope things get better ")
```

```
else:
    print("You seem pretty chill ")
    Boom! Your first sentiment-based chatbot
```

Translate with TextBlob

```
blob = TextBlob("Hello, I love AI.")
    translated = blob.translate(to='fr')
    print(translated)
    It speaks French now...
```

CHAPTER X

Computer Vision in Code

When AI Opens Its Eyes, Things Get Wild

You've made your AI read text, detect moods, even translate languages. Now let's upgrade its superpower level and teach it to see like a machine.

Welcome to Computer Vision — where AI looks at images and tries to make sense of what it's looking at.

Tools You'll Need

We'll use:

OpenCV – for loading and manipulating images

Matplotlib – for displaying images in Colab

In Colab: !pip install opencv-python-headless matplotlib

Loading an Image

First, upload a file (like cat.jpg) in Colab's left sidebar.

```
import cv2
import matplotlib.pyplot as plt
img = cv2.imread("cat.jpg")
img = cv2.cvtColor(img, cv2.COLOR_BGR2RGB)
plt.imshow(img)
plt.axis('off')
plt.show()
```

Boom. You've just loaded and displayed an image using Python.

Understanding What the Image Really Is

```
print("Image shape:", img.shape)
```

Output might be:

(400, 600, 3)

That means:

- 400 pixels tall
- 600 pixels wide
- 3 color channels (Red, Green, Blue)

Yup. AI sees images as arrays of numbers. Literally just... *math art.*

Convert to Grayscale

```
gray = cv2.cvtColor(img, cv2.COLOR_RGB2GRAY)
    plt.imshow(gray, cmap='gray')
    plt.axis('off')
    plt.show()
```

Why grayscale? It reduces complexity. Sometimes AI just needs shapes and contrast, not colors.

Crop, Resize, and Save

```
cropped = img[50:250, 100:300] # y1:y2, x1:x2
    resized = cv2.resize(img, (224, 224))
    cv2.imwrite("resized_cat.jpg",                cv2.cvtColor(resized,
cv2.COLOR_RGB2BGR))
```

Now you're preparing data like a pro. These steps are used before training models!

Edge Detection = Feature Detection

Let's find the important lines and edges:

```
    edges = cv2.Canny(gray, 100, 200)
    plt.imshow(edges, cmap='gray')
    plt.axis('off')
    plt.title("Edges Detected")
    plt.show()
```

These outlines help AI recognize shapes like faces, animals, or traffic signs.

Mini Project: Cartoonify Your Image

```
blurred = cv2.medianBlur(gray, 5)
    edges = cv2.adaptiveThreshold(
    blurred, 255, cv2.ADAPTIVE_THRESH_MEAN_C,
    cv2.THRESH_BINARY, 9, 10)
    plt.imshow(edges, cmap='gray')
    plt.axis('off')
    plt.title("Cartoon Filter")
    plt.show()
    Try it on your selfie or a friend's pic
```

CHAPTER XI

The AI Project Cycle (Idea ⇢ Reality)

How to Build an AI Project Like a Pro (Without Crying Into Your Code)

Building an AI project isn't just about throwing code at data and hoping for magic. It's a journey — a repeatable cycle. And if you follow the steps, you'll:

- Avoid chaos
- Build better stuff
- Impress anyone watching

Let's walk through the 6 classic stages of the AI project cycle.

Step 1: Problem Definition

"Wait... what are we even trying to solve?"
Before you write a single line of code, ask:

- What's the goal?
- Who's it for?
- What will the output be?

Example:
"I want to build a model that predicts whether someone is likely to have diabetes based on health data."

Step 2: Data Collection

"No data? No AI."
This is where you gather the information your AI needs to learn.
Data can be:

- Text (Tweets, reviews, transcripts)
- Tables (CSV files with numbers)
- Images (Faces, objects, handwriting)

- Audio (Speech, music)

Sources:

- Kaggle
- UCI ML Repository
- APIs (like Twitter or Reddit)
- Your own surveys or recordings

Step 3: Data Preparation

"Messy data = messy AI."
  Now you clean the mess. This step matters more than people realize.
  Includes:

- Handling missing values
- Normalizing or scaling data
- Tokenizing text
- Converting labels (like "Yes" → 1, "No" → 0)

  Tools:

- pandas, NumPy
- sklearn.preprocessing
- nltk for text

Step 4: Model Building

"Let the learning begin."
  This is where your machine starts learning patterns from the data.
  You pick:

- A model (like Decision Tree, Logistic Regression, Random Forest, etc.)
- Your features (inputs) and labels (outputs)

  Use: model.fit(X_train, y_train)

AI is officially learning. ??

Step 5: Evaluation

"Okay, but... how smart is it?"
You test your model on new data it hasn't seen before.
Metrics to check:

* Accuracy (for classification)
* Precision, Recall, F1 Score (for imbalanced datasets)
* Mean Squared Error (for regression)

Use:
from sklearn.metrics import classification_report
print(classification_report(y_test, y_pred))
This tells you if your model is a genius, or just confidently wrong. ?

Step 6: Deployment (Optional but Epic)

"Make it real. Let the world use it."
If your model works well — show it off! You can:

* Share a Colab notebook
* Build a Gradio or Streamlit app
* Convert it to a web API
* Add it to a website or app

Cool bonus tools:

* gradio.app – UI for models
* streamlit.io – Web app builder
* Hugging Face Spaces – Share your AI app with the world

CHAPTER XII

Project: Predicting Disease with AI

Teaching Machines to Diagnose (Almost Like a Doctor... But Not Quite)

Use Case: Predicting Diabetes

We'll use a public dataset — the Pima Indian Diabetes Dataset — with health info like:

- Glucose level
- BMI
- Blood pressure
- Age

...to predict whether a patient is likely diabetic (1) or not (0).

Dataset Link:

You can download it from Kaggle or use this simplified version: https://www.kaggle.com/datasets/uciml/pima-indians-diabetes-database

```
Pregnancies,Glucose,BloodPressure,SkinThickness,
Insulin,BMI,DiabetesPedigreeFunction,Age,Outcome
6,148,72,35,0,33.6,0.627,50,1
1,85,66,29,0,26.6,0.351,31,0
...
```

Step-by-Step Code (Explained Like a Friend)

1. Load Libraries + Data

```python
import pandas as pd
from sklearn.model_selection import train_test_split
from sklearn.ensemble import RandomForestClassifier
from sklearn.metrics import classification_report, accuracy_score
df = pd.read_csv("diabetes.csv")
print(df.head())
```

2. Features & Labels

```
X = df.drop("Outcome", axis=1) # Everything except the answer
    y = df["Outcome"] # The 'has diabetes' label
```

3. Train/Test Split

```
X_train, X_test, y_train, y_test = train_test_split(X, y, test_size=0.2,
random_state=42)
```

4. Train a Random Forest

```
model = RandomForestClassifier(n_estimators=100)
    model.fit(X_train, y_train)
```

5. Make Predictions

```
y_pred = model.predict(X_test)
    print("Accuracy:", accuracy_score(y_test, y_pred))
    print(classification_report(y_test, y_pred))
```

6. Visualize Feature Importance

```
import matplotlib.pyplot as plt
    importances = model.feature_importances_
    features = X.columns
    plt.figure(figsize=(10, 6))
    plt.barh(features, importances)
    plt.xlabel("Importance")
    plt.title("Which features matter most?")
    plt.show()
```

Mini Challenge:

Train a model to predict:

- Heart disease? (Try the Heart Disease UCI dataset)
- Parkinson's?
- Breast cancer?

Let them explore healthcare AI responsibly with a disclaimer:
This is an educational example. Real medical AI models are reviewed by experts and tested for safety. Never diagnose anyone with code from this book.

CHAPTER XIII

The Secret Shortcut!

Why Build from Scratch When the AI Brains Are Already Built?

Here's the truth: training your own AI model from zero can take:

* Days
* Weeks
* A beefy GPU
* Enough data to drown a cloud server

So what do smart devs (like you) do?
They borrow brains.
Welcome to the world of pretrained models — smart AIs trained on massive datasets, ready for you to use in seconds.

What Is a Pretrained Model?

A pretrained model is:

* Already trained on tons of data
* Already knows how to solve certain problems
* Ready for you to use or fine-tune for your needs

Think of it like:

* Using Google Translate instead of building your own translation system
* Applying an Instagram filter instead of coding image effects pixel-by-pixel.

Tools of the Trade

We'll explore two main tools:

Hugging Face

- A library with thousands of pretrained NLP models:
- Sentiment analysis
- Translation
- Summarization
- Text generation (yes, like ChatGPT!)

Google Teachable Machine

- A super beginner-friendly, drag-and-drop site for training CV models (image/audio/pose):
- Train by showing it pictures
- Export the model to use in Python or JavaScript

Hugging Face in Action: Sentiment Analyzer

Install the Transformers library (if needed):

```
!pip install transformers
```

Now load a model in just two lines:

```
from transformers import pipeline
sentiment_analyzer = pipeline("sentiment-analysis")
print(sentiment_analyzer("I love learning AI with this book!"))
```

Output:

```
[{'label': 'POSITIVE', 'score': 0.999}]
```

It's that simple. The model's been trained on thousands of reviews and can now read tone like a pro.

Try This:

Change the sentence to something sad, angry, sarcastic — see how it responds.

Teachable Machine (No Code Magic)

? Go to: teachablemachine.withgoogle.com
Steps:

- Choose Image Project
- Create 2 classes (e.g., "Mask" vs "No Mask", or "Happy" vs "Sad")
- Upload sample images or use webcam
- Train the model right in your browser

Export:

- TensorFlow → use in Python
- JavaScript → use on a website!

Perfect for:

- Rock-paper-scissors games
- Emotion detection
- Hand gesture recognition

Mini Project: Emotion Classifier

Use Teachable Machine to build:

- A webcam model that classifies facial expressions as "Happy", "Neutral", or "Sad"
- Export it
- Run it with a webcam app in Python or JS

Want to do it in Python? Here's the extra credit route ?

Why This Matters?

Pretrained models help you:

- Save time
- Skip hard math
- Build advanced projects faster
- Focus on what you want to create, not reinventing the wheel

CHAPTER XIV

Project: Fashion Trend Classifier

Teaching AI to Recognize Fashion Vibes from Product Names

Project Summary:

- Use product titles from the dataset (like "Men's Blue Denim Jeans")
- Predict which fashion trend or category they belong to
- Optional: Visualize which styles are most popular

Step-by-Step Plan:

1. Download and Load the Dataset

From Kaggle.
Download the file: styles.csv
   This CSV contains:

- id — product ID
- gender — male/female/unisex
- masterCategory — main category (Apparel, Accessories, etc.)
- subCategory — smaller category (Tshirts, Shirts, Dresses, etc.)
- articleType — article type (Jeans, Topwear, Saree, etc.)
- baseColour, season, usage, and productDisplayName

2.Load and Clean the Data

```
import pandas as pd
   # Load
   df = pd.read_csv('styles.csv', on_bad_lines='skip')
   # Clean
```

```
df = df.dropna(subset=['productDisplayName', 'subCategory'])
# Feature and label
X = df['productDisplayName']
y = df['subCategory']
```

3. Split into Train/Test

```
from sklearn.model_selection import train_test_split
    X_train, X_test, y_train, y_test = train_test_split(X, y, test_size=0.2,
random_state=42)
```

4.Text Vectorization (TF-IDF)

```
from sklearn.feature_extraction.text import TfidfVectorizer
    vectorizer = TfidfVectorizer(max_features=5000)
    X_train_vect = vectorizer.fit_transform(X_train)
    X_test_vect = vectorizer.transform(X_test)
    Now we're ready to train the models!
```

5.Model: Random Forest Classifier

```
from sklearn.ensemble import RandomForestClassifier
    from sklearn.metrics import accuracy_score, classification_report
    # Initialize and train
    rf_model          =          RandomForestClassifier(n_estimators=100,
random_state=42)
    rf_model.fit(X_train_vect, y_train)
    # Predict
    rf_pred = rf_model.predict(X_test_vect)
    # Evaluate
    print("Random Forest Accuracy:", accuracy_score(y_test, rf_pred))
    print(classification_report(y_test, rf_pred))
    Random Forest should do really well because it's good with text features.
    Accuracy: 99%
```

Code to Predict from User Input:

1. Take input from user

user_input = input("Enter a fashion product name: ")

2. Transform the input using the SAME vectorizer

user_input_vect = vectorizer.transform([user_input]) # note: input must be inside a list

3. Predict the subcategory

prediction = rf_model.predict(user_input_vect)

4. Show the result

print("Predicted Fashion Subcategory:", prediction[0]

Prediction:

```
        Enter a fashion product name: skinny fit jeans
But!    Predicted Fashion Subcategory: Bottomwear

        Enter a fashion product name: hat
        Predicted Fashion Subcategory: Shoes
```

A Quick Reality Check: How AI Actually Learns

As you can see — sometimes our AI nails it:
"skinny fit jeans" → Bottomwear
(Perfect prediction!)
    But other times, it can get hilariously confused:
"hat" → Shoes
(Wait, what?!)
    AI models don't really "understand" fashion like humans do. They simply learn patterns from the data they've seen. If they haven't seen enough examples of something (like hats), they might guess wrong — and still

sound confident!

And that's okay.

That's normal in the world of AI.

Refer to Appendix for more

Exploring the Cloud — AWS Essentials

"You've built skills. Now let's make them global."

In this part, you'll learn how to use the real engines that power the internet: Cloud computing and AWS.

Launch servers, train models, store data — all in the cloud, and all by YOU.

CHAPTER XV

AWS — Your First Step Into the Cloud

What is AWS?

AWS = Amazon Web Services.

It's Amazon's cloud computing platform.

Instead of running programs or saving files on your computer, AWS lets you do it over the internet ("the cloud").

Big Idea: You pay for what you use — like ordering electricity, not buying a whole power plant.

Example: Hosting a website, training an AI model, storing photos.

Why Everyone Loves the Cloud (especially AWS)

- Speed: Launch servers or storage in minutes
- Pay-as-You-Go: Only pay for what you actually use
- Scalability: Handle 10 visitors or 10 million easily
- Security: Encrypted, certified, trusted by banks & Netflix!
- Global Access: Servers everywhere around the world

What Can You Actually Do With AWS?

- Host websites
- Store huge files
- Train AI and ML models
- Run apps without buying servers
- Create databases
- Build games
- Backup your phone automatically

Important AWS Services You Must Know

- EC2: Virtual computers ("instances")
- S3: Cloud storage for any file
- RDS: Managed database service (MySQL, PostgreSQL)
- Lambda: Run code without servers ("serverless")
- SageMaker: Build, train, and deploy ML models
- CloudFront: Super fast content delivery (CDN)
- IAM: Manage users, passwords, permissions

How AWS Works (The Quick Story)

Step 1: You create an AWS account (free tier available)
Step 2: You pick a service (like EC2 to create a server)
Step 3: You configure it (choose server size, storage)
Step 4: AWS launches it in a datacenter
Step 5: You access it through the AWS Management Console or CLI
    Simple idea: Rent computers, storage, or services from Amazon instead of buying your own.

Quick Tour: How to Launch Your First Server (EC2)

- Log into AWS Console.
- Click EC2.
- Launch a new instance.
- Choose an OS (Amazon Linux, Ubuntu, Windows).
- Choose a free-tier eligible instance type (t2.micro).
- Configure security (open port 22 for SSH).
- Launch and connect!

Congratulations: You just rented a computer on the internet!

AWS Tools You Should Try (No-Code to Pro Level)

- AWS Management Console: Web interface (click around)
- AWS CLI: Command-line for serious builders
- AWS Cloud9: Cloud coding IDE (write code in browser!)
- SageMaker Studio: Full AI/ML environment

Machine Learning on AWS (SageMaker Mini Intro)

- Prebuilt ML models ready to use
- Easy model training on big datasets
- Deploy models instantly as APIs

You could build:

- Image classifiers
- Chatbots
- Predictive models ...without buying GPUs yourself!

CHAPTER XVI

Project: Build a Simple AWS Chatbot (Lex + Lambda)

What Are We Building?

A chatbot that can answer simple questions (like "Hello", "What's your name?", "Bye")
Using Amazon Lex (AWS service for building chatbots)
Use Lambda function to add smart backend replies
What You Need First:
AWS account (free-tier eligible)
IAM permissions for Lex and Lambda
Basic idea for your chatbot (let's build a simple "Friendly Bot")

Step-by-Step Process

1. Create a Lex Bot (the chatbot brain)

Go to AWS Management Console → Search for Lex → Open Amazon Lex V2
Click "Create Bot"
Fill Details:

- Bot name: FriendlyBot
- IAM role: Let AWS create one automatically
- Children directed? Choose "No" (simple flow)
- Languages: English (en-US)

Click "Next"

2. Create Intents (Chatbot understanding)

Intent = What the user wants to say or ask.
Create 2 Intents:

Intent 1: Greeting

Name: GreetIntent
Sample utterances:

- "Hello"
- "Hi"
- "Hey"

Response: "Hi there! How can I help you today?"

Intent 2: Goodbye

Name: ByeIntent
Sample utterances:

- "Bye"
- "See you"
- "Goodbye"

Response: "Goodbye! Have a great day ahead!"
Save each Intent.
Build your bot (button on top).
Click "Test Bot" → Say "Hi" → Bot should answer!

3. Add Lambda Function (to make smart replies)

Lambda = Small cloud function that can run custom code.
Go to AWS Lambda → Click Create Function
Choose:

- Author from Scratch
- Name: FriendlyBotHandler
- Runtime: Python 3.9

Create function

4. Write Simple Lambda Function Code

Inside Lambda function editor, replace code with:

```
# Simple dynamic response

    user_message = event['inputTranscript']

    if 'weather' in user_message.lower():

        reply = "The weather is great today!"

    elif 'name' in user_message.lower():

        reply = "I'm FriendlyBot, your assistant."

    else:

        reply = "Sorry, I didn't understand. Can you rephrase
it?"

    return {

        "sessionState": {

            "dialogAction": {

                "type": "Close"

            },

            "intent": {

                "name":
event['sessionState']['intent']['name'],

                "state": "Fulfilled"

            }

        },

        "messages": [
```

```
{

    "contentType": "PlainText",

    "content": reply

}

]

}
```

Deploy function (Save + Deploy button)

5. *Connect Lambda to Lex*

- Go back to your Lex Bot → Settings → Lambda functions
- Attach your FriendlyBotHandler Lambda function to the bot.
- Assign Lambda under each intent if needed.
- Build the Bot again
- Test the Bot again!

6. *Test Full Chatbot*

- Type "Hi" → Bot says hello.
- Type "What's your name?" → Lambda responds dynamically.
- Type "How's the weather?" → Lambda responds dynamically.
- Type "Bye" → Bot says goodbye.

You just built a real chatbot on AWS!

Appendix: Fashion Trend Classifier Model — Full Code Explanation

1. Importing Libraries and Loading the Dataset

import pandas as pd

pandas is a Python library used to work with data stored in tables (like spreadsheets).

It helps us read, clean, and manipulate CSV files easily.

df = pd.read_csv('styles.csv', on_bad_lines='skip')

This reads the styles.csv file into a DataFrame called df.

on_bad_lines='skip' tells pandas to ignore any badly formatted rows (errors).

2. Cleaning the Data

df = df.dropna(subset=['productDisplayName', 'subCategory'])

dropna() removes any rows where productDisplayName or subCategory is missing.

Without these, we cannot train the AI because we'd be missing either input text or labels.

3. Preparing Features and Labels

X = df['productDisplayName']

y = df['subCategory']

- X (input): the product names — the text that AI will learn from.
- y (output): the categories like "T-shirt", "Jeans", etc. — the answers that AI will try to predict.

4. Splitting Data into Training and Testing Sets

from sklearn.model_selection import train_test_split

X_train, X_test, y_train, y_test = train_test_split(X, y, test_size=0.2, random_state=42)

We split the data:

- 80% for training (to learn from)
- 20% for testing (to check if AI really learned)
- random_state=42 makes the split reproducible — same results every time.

5. Converting Text into Numbers (TF-IDF Vectorization)

```
from sklearn.feature_extraction.text import TfidfVectorizer
    vectorizer = TfidfVectorizer(max_features=5000)
    X_train_vect = vectorizer.fit_transform(X_train)
    X_test_vect = vectorizer.transform(X_test)
    AI can't understand text directly.
```
We use TF-IDF (Term Frequency-Inverse Document Frequency) to:

- Count important words
- Convert text into numbers that represent meaning
- max_features=5000 limits it to 5000 most important words for faster processing.

6. Building the Random Forest Classifier Model

```
from sklearn.ensemble import RandomForestClassifier
    from sklearn.metrics import accuracy_score, classification_report
    Random Forest is a collection of decision trees — it makes predictions
by majority voting.
    # Initialize and train
    rf_model          =          RandomForestClassifier(n_estimators=100,
random_state=42)
    rf_model.fit(X_train_vect, y_train)
```

- n_estimators=100 means 100 trees in the forest.
- fit() means "learn from training data."

7. Predicting and Evaluating the Model

# Predict
    rf_pred = rf_model.predict(X_test_vect)
    Here, we ask our trained AI model to guess the subcategories on test data it hasn't seen before.
    # Evaluate
    print("Random Forest Accuracy:", accuracy_score(y_test, rf_pred))
    print(classification_report(y_test, rf_pred))

- accuracy_score gives overall how often the AI was right.
- classification_report gives detailed stats like precision, recall, and F1-score for each class.

8. Predicting a New Fashion Item Entered by User

# 1. Take input from user
    user_input = input("Enter a fashion product name: ")
    Asks user to type a product name like "Slim Fit Black Shirt".
    # 2. Transform the input using the SAME vectorizer
    user_input_vect = vectorizer.transform([user_input]) # inside list []
    Transforms the user's sentence into TF-IDF numeric format, exactly like training data.
    # 3. Predict the subcategory
    prediction = rf_model.predict(user_input_vect)
    AI predicts what kind of fashion item it is (e.g., "Shirt", "Topwear").
    # 4. Show the result
    print("Predicted Fashion Subcategory:", prediction[0])
    Nicely prints out the predicted fashion category to the user.

Let's Connect!

If you loved this book, have feedback, found any mistakes (oops!), or just want to talk about AI and future tech —
I'd love to hear from you!
    Email: adhyayantiwari7@gmail.com
    LinkedIn: Adhyayan Tiwari
    Instagram: @heyaiwhatsup
    Let's keep learning and building together!

Closing Thoughts

Hey you — yeah, you, the one still reading.

By now, you've learned how AI thinks, learns, sees, talks, and even dreams a little bit.

You've coded, explored, built, imagined, and maybe even laughed along the way.

But here's the real truth:

The future of AI isn't written yet.

It's still being drawn, sketched, and coded by people like you — the dreamers who dare to ask:

"What else is possible?"

AI isn't about replacing humans.

It's about amplifying humanity — our kindness, our creativity, our dreams, and our crazy what-if ideas.

This book was never just about machines learning from humans.

It was about humans learning from machines — to be more curious, more patient, more unstoppable.

So go ahead — Break things. Build things. Imagine things.

The future is wide open. And it's waiting for you.

– Adhyayan Tiwari

P.S. If you invent a real Doraemon... remember me, okay?